HOW TO DRIVE AN INDY RACE CAR

MASTERS OF MOTION

DAVID RUBEL

ILLUSTRATED BY GREGORY TRUETT SMITH, JIM FINNELL, AND CHRIS BRIGMAN
PHOTOGRAPHY BY EDWARD KEATING

Acknowledgments:

We would like to thank Al Unser, Jr., Bob Walters, and the rest of the Galles-Kraco team for their active and generous support of this project.

John Muir Publications, P.O. Box 613, Santa Fe, NM 87504

First edition. First printing

Library of Congress Cataloging-in-Publication Data

Rubel, David.
　　How to drive an Indy race car / David Rubel ; photography by
Edward Keating ; illustrations by Jim Finnell, Gregory Truett Smith,
Chris Brigman. — 1st ed.
　　　p.　cm. — (Masters of motion)
　　Includes index.
　　Summary: Al Unser, Jr. places the reader in the driver's seat of
an Indy race car while explaining how the design of the car affects
performance and safety, and how scientific principles guide drivers
in racing strategy.
　　ISBN 1-56261-045-7 (hardcover). — ISBN 1-56261-062-7 (paper)
　　1. Automobiles, Racing— Juvenile literature. 2. Automobile
racing— Juvenile literature.　[1. Automobiles, Racing.
2. Automobile racing.]　I. Keating, Edward, ill.　II. Title.
III. Series.
TL236.R83　1992
796.7'2— dc20　　　　　　　　　　　　　　　　92-4545
　　　　　　　　　　　　　　　　　　　　　　　　　　CIP
　　　　　　　　　　　　　　　　　　　　　　　　　　AC

Consultants: Agincourt Press
Design: Ken Wilson
Illustrations: James Finnell, Gregory Truett Smith, Chris Brigman
Typography: Ken Wilson
Printer: Worzalla
Photographs by Edward Keating,except photograph on title page,
　courtesy of Valvoline; photograph on page 15, courtesy of Skip
　Barber Racing School; photograph on page 35, courtesy of Ron
　McQueeney, Indy 500 Photos.
Drawing of engine on page 9 courtesy of Chevrolet.

Distributed to the book trade by
W.W. Norton, Inc.
New York, New York

Distributed to the education market by
The Wright Group
19201 120th Avenue NE
Bothell, WA 98011

What's going on here? The next thing I know I'm strapped into an Indy race car that's traveling nearly 200 miles per hour. The entire car is pounding like a jackhammer. The engine is shrieking. It's close to 150°F inside the driver's cockpit, and it seems even hotter inside this helmet. I have no idea what I'm doing. And here comes a turn!

Don't panic. Just listen. Pull to the outside. Brake while you're still on the straightaway. Trail brakes into the turn. Then squeeze power.

"What? Who's that? Who's talking to me?"

Talk later. Brake now. At 200 miles per hour, you don't have much time.

"O.K., I'm braking."

Now turn.

"I'm turning. But I'm still going fast, too fast."

Don't—

"I better brake some more."

—brake.

"How interesting. My rear wheels are moving out past the front ones. Yow, I'm spinning!"

Turn in the direction of the spin!

"What do you mean turn? I'm spinning."

Step on the clutch. Step on the brakes. All the way! Lock it in! Lock it in!

SCREECH! *That was close. How did I get on the infield grass, though? Everything seems to be all right. The car seems O.K. I seem O.K. Even the engine is still running. But there's that voice in my ear again. Maybe I'm hallucinating.*

Next time, remember, you've got to brake on the straightaway, then trail, or ease up on, the brakes as you turn. Don't add brakes after you've started to turn. If you do that, you'll shift too much weight onto the front wheels and mess up the car's balance. That's why you dropped wheels.

"Dropped wheels?"

Right, dropped wheels. Exceeded the vertical load. Spun out.

AL UNSER, JR.

Al—or Junior, as he's known on pit row—has just about done it all. He started racing sprint cars at the age of 16, drove his first Indy car at 20, and won his first Indy race just two years later.

Between 1984 and 1989, Junior won eight more races and earned purses worth over $4,000,000. Then, in 1990, he had the greatest single year of his career, winning six times for Galles-Kraco Racing on his way to the IndyCar championship and $1,946,833 in prize money. Along the way, Al set a record at the Michigan 500 for the fastest 500-mile race ever. Including pit stops, his average speed was 189.727 miles per hour.

Just about the only thing that Al hadn't done was win the Indy 500. His father—Al, Sr.—won there four times, and his uncle Bobby three. But it wasn't until 1992 that Little Al finally took the checkered flag at Indianapolis, winning by less than a car length in the closest 500 finish ever.

"Who are you? Where are you?"

I'm Al Unser, Jr., Indy racing champion, hard-charger, and all-around nice guy. Right now, I'm in pit row, which is where you should be.

"How can I hear you if you're in the pit?"

There are tiny speakers built into the earplugs inside your helmet. There's also a microphone built into your helmet's chin padding. A small radio mounted under your legs lets us communicate back and forth. It uses the forward antenna on the nose.

Now, shift the car into gear, and bring it on down to the pit. Slowly. We've got a lot to talk about before you get back on the track again.

CHECKING OUT THE CAR

"O.K., Al, where do I park?" See the T-marks on the pavement? Stop there. Now climb on out, and we'll take a look at what you've been driving.

"This car's a lot smaller than I expected. It looks more like an oversize go-cart than a race car."

Well, looks can be deceiving. The Indy car is the fastest racer there is. But it's true. The car is small. That's because there's nothing on the body that doesn't need to be there. Making the car's body more compact means less drag, or air resistance, out on the track. And less drag translates directly into speed.

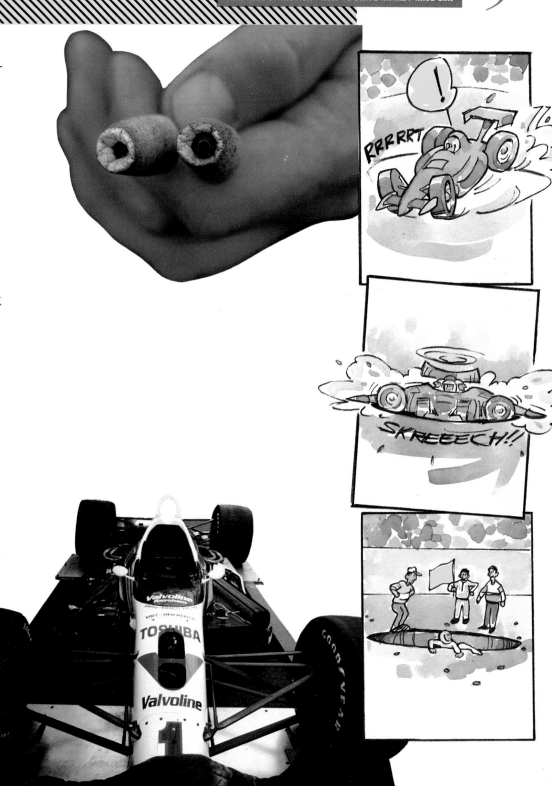

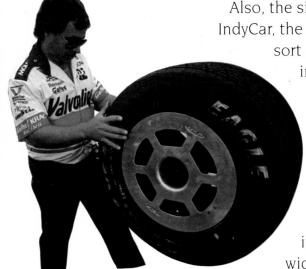

Also, the size of the car is regulated by IndyCar, the sanctioning body for Indy racing, sort of like the commissioner's office in baseball or the NFL in football. According to the rules, no Indy car can be more than 15 feet 5 inches long or 6 feet 6½ inches wide measured from the outside edges of the wheel rims. The bullet-shaped part of the car in which the driver sits—it's called the tub—is limited to a width of 22½ inches.

"How much does an Indy car weigh?"

The rules require that each unfueled car weigh at least 1,550 pounds, not counting the driver.

"That doesn't seem like very much."

It's not. A typical two-door sports car weighs in the neighborhood of 2,500 pounds. But we'd go even lighter than 1,550 pounds if we could, because the lighter the car, the faster it goes. And in this game, fast is everything.

Let's do a walkaround, and I'll point out some of the car's more important design features.

Indy Tires

We can start with the tires. First of all, they're wider and heavier than a passenger car's. And the rear tires are even wider and heavier than the front ones.

"They're also completely bald. Has the tread been worn off?"

No, they're almost brand-new. Dry tires are supposed to look like that. It's rain tires that have the type of grooved tread you're used to seeing on passenger cars. But we only use rain tires when the racing surface is wet. Otherwise, we use dry tires because they stick better, and being completely flat, they put more surface area on the road. That gives the car better grip.

"Then why not use dry tires all the time?"

Because on wet surfaces, a cushion of water sometimes forms between the tires and the track, which can cause the tires to lose their grip. If that happens, you'll almost definitely spin out on the next turn. The grooves in rain tires work against this by channeling the water away from the contact patches between the tires and the ground.

"What are all these pebbles doing set into the tires? Are they built into the tread to help grip the road?"

No, the tires just pick them up during heat cycling. Sticker tires—

"Sticker tires?"

New tires. Ones with the manufacturer's sticker still on them. They come perfectly smooth. Then we take them out onto the track and heat cycle them.

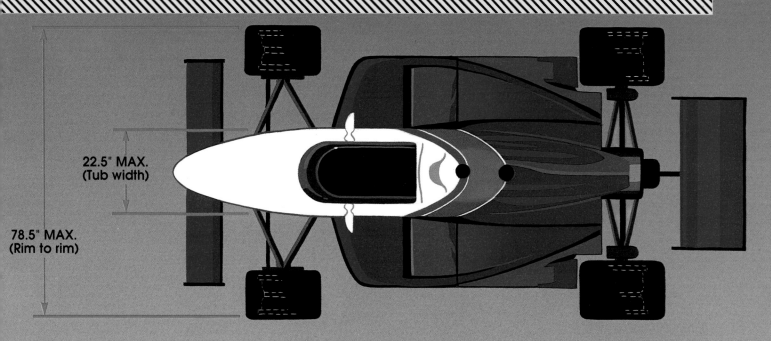

22.5" MAX.
(Tub width)

78.5" MAX.
(Rim to rim)

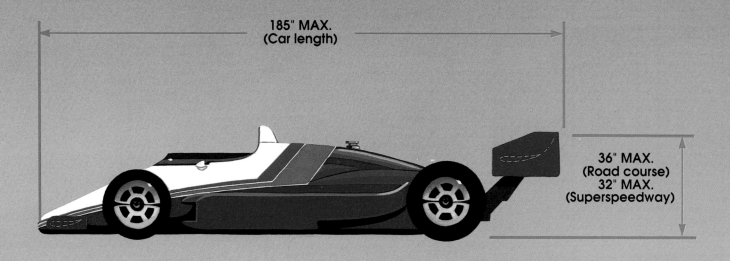

185" MAX.
(Car length)

36" MAX.
(Road course)
32" MAX.
(Superspeedway)

INDY CAR DIMENSIONS

UNDERWING

That means we slowly bring them up to racing temperature, usually about 240°F, and run them hot for a few laps. Heat cycling the tires twice cures them at that temperature. Without heat cycling, new tires tend to heat up too quickly during a race, and that can cause blistering.

Indy car dashboards use the same liquid crystal displays that watches and calculators do. The read-outs can be configured to show the driver everything from engine rpm and oil pressure to battery voltage and coolant temperature.

"And the pebbles?"

At 240°F, the rubber in the tires gets a little sticky and tends to pick up whatever is loose on the track. If you ever see a completely smooth set of tires, you know they're not ready yet for racing.

"O.K., I've got the tires. What's next?"

Actually, I've given you just a simple rundown on the tires. The engineering that goes into them—into everything about these cars—is a lot more complicated than most people think. For example, let's take a look at some of the special design features that help keep Indy car tires on the race track.

The Wings

The long, flat piece that hangs down across the front of the car is called the front wing. It works like an upside-down airplane wing.

REAR WING

Superspeedway

Road course

Because it's upside down, the wing pushes the car down against the track, instead of lifting it up. This action is called downforce. The front wing also directs the air over and under the car. The airflow under the car creates additional downforce called ground effects.

"Which are?"

Kneel down and take a peek under the car. What you're looking at is called the underwing. See those tunnels? As air passes through them at high speed, they create a partial vacuum under the car.

"Which sucks the car to the track?"

Exactly. At 175 miles per hour, the wings and the ground effects will produce an additional downforce equal to 1.5 times the force of gravity. That means the 1,550-pound car will hug the track as though it weighs 3,875 pounds.

"I'm not sure I'm clear on that."

O.K., think about it this way: Indy cars generate so much aerodynamic downforce, compared to their weight, that you could run one upside down on a ceiling. The partial vacuum under the car, combined with the inverted airplane wings, would make the car stick.

"Not on my ceiling."

Have it your way. But you'll need every ounce of that downforce to hold your line through some of these turns as fast as you'll be taking them. The more downforce on the wheels, the better they'll corner. We'd like to get even more, but there are rules against it.

"You mean there are rules that make you go slower?"

Actually, most of the rules are designed to make the cars go slower. IndyCar worries that if we go too fast, the cars won't be crashworthy. So the rules committee comes up with different ways to limit the cars' performance. With every new rule, though, it becomes the job of each race team to find ways to go faster despite the limitations. It's the engineers' success or failure at this that gives each team its competitive edge. Because almost everybody uses the same cars and the same engines and the same tires, it's how you adapt your equipment that really makes the difference between winning and losing.

"Winning and losing, right. I'm with you. Is that it for the wings?"

Front wing and underwing, yes. The rear wings, no. There are two types of rear wing. The 36-inch-high wing that's on the car now is used for road courses and the slower ovals. On superspeedways, like Indianapolis and the Michigan International Speedway, we use a smaller, single-element design that's only 32 inches high.

"Why use a smaller wing?"

Because on really fast ovals, where the straightaways are long and every turn is a gimme, the smaller wing exchanges downforce, which you don't need, for less drag, which helps you go faster.

"Why don't you need the downforce?"

Because the turns are easy. And because at 225 miles per hour, the car's ground effects are already delivering more than enough stick.

FRONT WING

REAR WING

SIDE WINGS

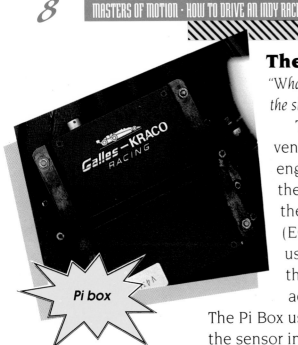

Pi box

The Nuts and Bolts

"What are these finlike extensions bolted to the sides of the tub?"

They're called sidepods. The vents in each one scoop air into the engine to help keep it cool. Behind the vent on the right sidepod are the Electronic Control Module (ECM) and the Pi Box. The ECM uses electronic sensors to check the performance of the car and adjust the fuel injection system. The Pi Box uses radio waves to communicate the sensor information—and more—to the crew in the pit.

"And that's what the second antenna on the nose of the car is for?"

Right, but I'll go into more detail about the onboard electronics later. For now, let's look at the sidepod on the driver's left. Behind its vent is an overflow tank. Just as in ordinary cars, Indy cars have pumps that circulate oil to keep their engines running smoothly. But often high Indy engine temperatures cause the oil to expand. Instead of spilling out onto the track, the oil moves from the main oil reservoir into the overflow tank, which also picks up the cornering slosh. The mechanics call it the puke tank.

"How colorful of them."

Above the left sidepod is the fuel intake. And above that, on top of the car—see that upside-down U? That's the rollover hoop. According to IndyCar rules, there must be at least 5 inches between the driver's helmet and an imaginary line drawn from the dashboard to the top of the hoop. The rollover hoop is so strong that it can support the entire weight of the car. Without it, the driver's head would have to do that job if the car were somehow to flip over.

"Which would hurt."

And also ruin a very expensive helmet.

"What makes the rollover hoop so strong? It looks like a simple piece of fiberglass to me."

No, not fiberglass. It's steel wrapped in carbon fiber, which is as strong as steel but only one-fifth the weight. The smoothness of the paint helps limit the air friction, but the shape of the rollover hoop is still Drag City.

The same thing happens to your body. Even in a passenger car, if you turn to the left, your body is pulled to the right. It's just that in Indy cars, the faster speeds make the pull stronger. If you weigh 150 pounds, then on each turn you'll feel the equivalent of a 450- to 600-pound weight pulling you to the right. That's why we tie your body down with seat belts and support your neck with the strap.

Seat Belts

"Those seat belts do look pretty substantial."

They're the standard six-point outfit. Two shoulder harnesses, two lap belts, and two antisubmarine belts, all joined together at a central quick-release buckle.

"What are antisubmarine belts? Some kind of weapons system?"

Climb in. I'll show you. Put your feet in first, then grab hold of the sides and slide your feet down toward the nose. That's right. Now buckle up tight. Comfortable?

"The seat's a little hard, but it feels O.K."

We're about the same size, so the seat should fit you pretty well. It was made to fit me exactly. I sat on a plastic bag filled with a fast-setting foam, which formed a mold of my back. Then the seat was made to fit that mold. The seat itself is carbon fiber, which is a very hard material. It feels comfortable to me, though, because its close fit distributes my weight and spreads all the vibrations of racing across my entire body, instead of just up my spine. That makes a big difference over a 500-mile race. Now, have you figured out what the antisubmarine belts are for?

"It's pretty obvious once you put them on. They keep the driver from sliding out of the seat, right?"

You got it. If you were to hit something—say, the wall—head on, the tendency would be for you to shoot right down into the nose of the car. The antisubmarine belts prevent that.

SAFETY GEAR

COCKPIT CONTROLS

Next, moving on to the cockpit controls, there's a small knob on your right attached to a lever just above your thigh. That's the gear shift. It controls the six forward gears.

"What about reverse?"

You don't need reverse on an oval because you never back up. In fact, on fast ovals, the only reason you need the first five gears is to get you into sixth, where you run flat out all race long. Try shifting through the gear pattern. You'll notice that the transmission handles just like a manual transmission in a normal passenger car, except that the gears are much closer together.

"Where's the speedometer?"

You don't need one during a race. It doesn't matter how fast you're going as long as it's faster than the car behind you.

"And the fuel gauge?"

A fuel gauge really isn't practical for an Indy car. The centrifugal force on turns pulls so much of the fuel to one side of the cell that you'd get misleading readings. Anyway, a fuel gauge could never be as pinpoint accurate as you need it to be. It's better to calculate the fuel remaining by keeping track of the fuel already used. Each lap, the Pi Box tells the engineers how many times the fuel injectors fired as well as how much fuel was released each time. From these numbers, the engineers can calculate fuel consumption to a very precise degree.

HOW TO BECOME AN INDY DRIVER

Indy car racing isn't exactly well suited to on-the-job training. The cost of fielding a team is so high that car owners need to be sure their drivers are the best around, the most talented and the most experienced.

But how do you find out whether you've got the talent? Where do you go to get the experience? Many Indy hopefuls turn to the Skip Barber Racing School in Canaan, Connecticut.

At the Skip Barber school, which offers programs at professional tracks all over the country, novice drivers can enroll in the same competition course that 1991 IndyCar champion Michael Andretti took when he was just starting out. The introductory training takes three days, during which professionals teach students the basics of race car driving. Exercises on the track include downshifting and trail-braking, while classroom sessions explain how to find the best line through a turn and how to control the weight shift of the car.

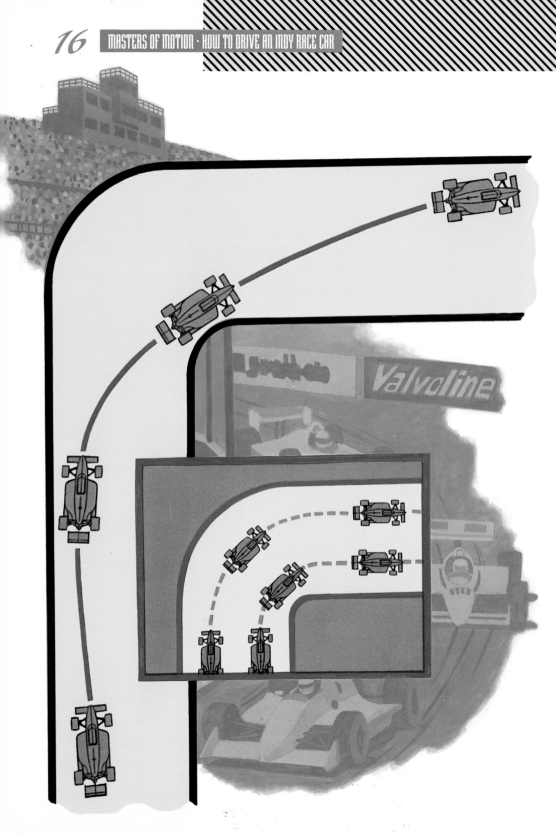

THE ART OF THE INDY TURN

All right. Now that we've covered the controls, it's time to give you some basic lessons in turning. Remember, racing is basically going very fast while turning. It's one thing to go 200 miles an hour on a straightaway and quite another to carry that speed through a turn.

You can break down every turn into three distinct parts: the turn-in point, the apex, and the track-out point. Entry, middle, and exit. The turn-in point is the place on the outside of the track where you first begin to turn. The apex is the point at which you clip the inside of the curve. And the track-out point is where you end up. Here. I'll diagram a classic 90-degree turn for you. You start on the outside of the track and end up on the outside, because that gives you the widest possible radius in which to turn.

"Why does the radius of the turn matter?"

Common sense tells you that a car can take a wide turn faster than a sharp one. But so does physics. When you're turning, there are three crucial factors you have to take into account: your speed going into the turn, your car's ability to grip the road, and the line you take through the turn.

"How do you know what line to take through the turn?"

There are a few different approaches. One is the constant radius arc. That means the line

At the end of the straightaway, I ease up on the throttle and let the car slow down for about two seconds before I turn and add power. Then the rear tires dig in, and I come shooting out of the corner even faster than I entered it.

And the next thing I see is another turn coming up on me much sooner than I expected. I let up on the throttle, turn the nose into the curve, and accelerate even harder. Al's right. The car handles better when I push it.

FLAGS

GREEN/*START:* Indicates the start of a race, or a restart after a yellow flag.

YELLOW/*CAUTION:* Indicates an unsafe condition, such as an accident, on the track. Drivers are required to slow down and maintain their position. Passing is not allowed, but cars may close up behind the leader.

RED/*STOP:* Indicates the stop of a race due to an unsafe condition.

BLACK/*PIT IMMEDIATELY:* Indicates that the car being signaled must pull into pit row immediately.

BLUE WITH A YELLOW DIAGONAL STRIPE/*MOVE TO ANOTHER LANE:* Indicates that a faster car is overtaking the car being signaled.

YELLOW WITH TWO VERTICAL RED BARS/*OIL ON THE TRACK:* Drivers are also warned of the location of the spill.

WHITE/*LAST LAP*

CHECKERED/*VICTORY*

IN THE PIT

*L*ook for the T-marks. Great. Stop right there and shut it down. While you're catching your breath, we're going to download some data from the Pi Box into a laptop computer. Then the engineers will analyze that data and tell the mechanics what adjustments to make. Jack it up, boys!

A few weeks before each race, we travel to the race site and run some test laps on the track to see how well the car handles. From those test laps, the engineers build a data record and then develop a ballpark setup specifically for each track. Now that you've run a few more laps, the team can start to fine-tune that setup. They'll measure the atmospheric conditions—air temperature, air viscosity—

"*Air viscosity?*"

Also known as air density. When engineers think about air, they like to think of it as a fluid. In that way, the front and rear wings act like the keel of a ship. The degree to which the air resists flowing past them, because of friction, is called its viscosity. Mercury has a low viscosity. Maple syrup has a high viscosity. Oil has a lower viscosity when it's warm than when it's cold. Anyway, we take all sorts of site conditions into account. If the track is hot on race day, for example, that can affect

Air jack

PIT STOP

:01—The car pulls into the pit and stops short, just in front of a crew-held placement sign.

:02—The air jack man and the fueler jump over the pit wall and race to the car.

:03—Four more crew members—one for each tire—grab air-powered impact wrenches and follow their teammates over the wall.

:04—The fueler locks the methanol nozzle into the car's fuel intake, called a bull's-eye, while the air jack man hooks up the compressed air hose that powers the jack.

:05—The chassis pops off the ground as the tire men spin off the single lug nut that locks each wheel in place. Other than the roar of the engines, the hammering of the wrenches is racing's most recognizable sound.

:06—Wheel-and-tire assemblies weighing more than 40 pounds are swept aside, revealing bare hubs that are covered almost instantly by new sets of tires.

:07—With the flick of a switch, the impact wrenches are reversed, and they chatter again as lug nuts spin back onto their mounts.

:08—The new tires are in place.

:09—Finished with their primary task, two tire men check the sidepod vents for debris and other possible obstructions, while the other two check the wings.

:10—The fuel cell is full.

:11—The fueler disconnects the coupling, which automatically reseals the cell.

:12—Tire changers frantically search for any loose equipment that might be scattered by the car as it leaves.

:13—The air jack man decouples the compressor hose and releases the jack. The car bounces back to the ground.

:14—Crew members move to the rear of the car for a push start in case the car stalls.

:15—The driver pulls out of the pit and rejoins the race.

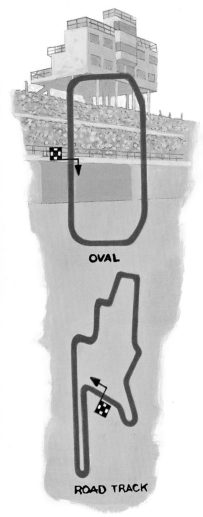

OVAL

ROAD TRACK

everything from coolant temperature to boost. We're running so close to the edge with this machine—in the top 1 percent of what it can do—that even the most minor adjustments can make a huge difference in performance and handling. Changing the wing angle by a single degree in the wrong direction, for instance, can cost you 10 miles per hour.

"It sounds like trying to sit on top of a bubble."

And we keep falling off, because conditions are constantly changing in minute ways from one lap to the next. But the longer you can ride that bubble, the faster you'll go and the better you'll do.

I've driven this car so many miles that I know it inside and out. I can tell how it's doing just by the feel of it. When I drive practice runs, I'm constantly talking to the engineers about how the car's handling and how the engine's performing. If the tires are slipping, or the wings are out of adjustment, or the suspension is loose and the car is oversteering, I pass that information along to the engineers. Then they tell the mechanics what adjustments to make to correct each problem.

Do me a favor. Climb up on the car and hop up and down on it. Now help us roll the car back and forth.

"What are we doing?"

Settling the car down before the crew takes some measurements to confirm the adjustments they've made.

More about Indy Tires

Now is probably a good time to tell you some more about the tires. Indy car tires have the same basic design as passenger car tires, but they use different rubber compounds for each race depending on the track surface, just as skiers use different waxes on their skis. Depending on the snow conditions, skiers use one wax for slopes covered in a fine powder and another for wet slush. The same goes for racing tires. Different compounds work better on different tracks. Some work better at

superspeedway speeds than at the slower road course speeds. Others corner better on concrete than on asphalt.

At the beginning of

each race weekend, Goodyear delivers either twenty-eight or forty-four tires to each team. We get seven sets for short ovals and road courses, the eleven sets for superspeedway events. The tires have been designed to produce the best possible performance on that weekend's track. Here, we'll practice with four sets and save three for the race, one set to start with and one for each of the two pit stops.

Top Performance

"So what's the bottom line, Al? Give me some performance specs. How fast can this car go?"

The fastest qualifying lap ever run by an Indy car was Emerson Fittipaldi's fourth lap at Indianapolis in 1990, when he ran the 2.5-mile oval in 39.898 seconds. That works out to an average speed of 225.575 miles per hour. But you know he was going faster than that on the straightaways, probably in the 230 to 235 mph range. In 1986, Rick Mears set an international record with a lap speed of 233.934 miles per hour during a practice session at the Michigan International Speedway.

Indy cars also have phenomenal acceleration. Driven by engines that put out close to 750 horsepower, Indy cars can do 0 to 100 miles per hour in just 4.5 seconds. In compari-

son, passenger cars typically operate in the 150-horsepower range. But instead of just hearing about it, why don't you climb back in and really start to push the car? Remember, these machines are set up to go fast, and they just won't work well at slower speeds. Don't be tentative. Push the car. Push yourself.

Driving these cars is all about nerve. You don't need great reflexes, great strength, or even great eyesight. What you need are competitiveness and nerve. You've got to be able to take the car right out to the edge, to floor the throttle and run right up to within an inch or two of the wall on the turns. Be fearless. I want to see you in sixth gear this time.

"Doesn't physical ability matter at all?"

Not the way it does in football or basketball. But you do have to be in shape. Drivers' heart rates, which are normally in the range of 75 beats per minute, can soar as high as 200 beats per minute, which is higher even than astronauts experience at launch. It's not unusual for a driver to keep a pulse of 150 beats per minute for the entire three hours of an Indianapolis 500. Plus there's dehydration to worry about. The cockpit heats up pretty good, even though it is open to the air. Drivers sweat so much that they can lose up to 6 percent of their total body weight during a 500-mile race. Here, take a drink, then get on after it.

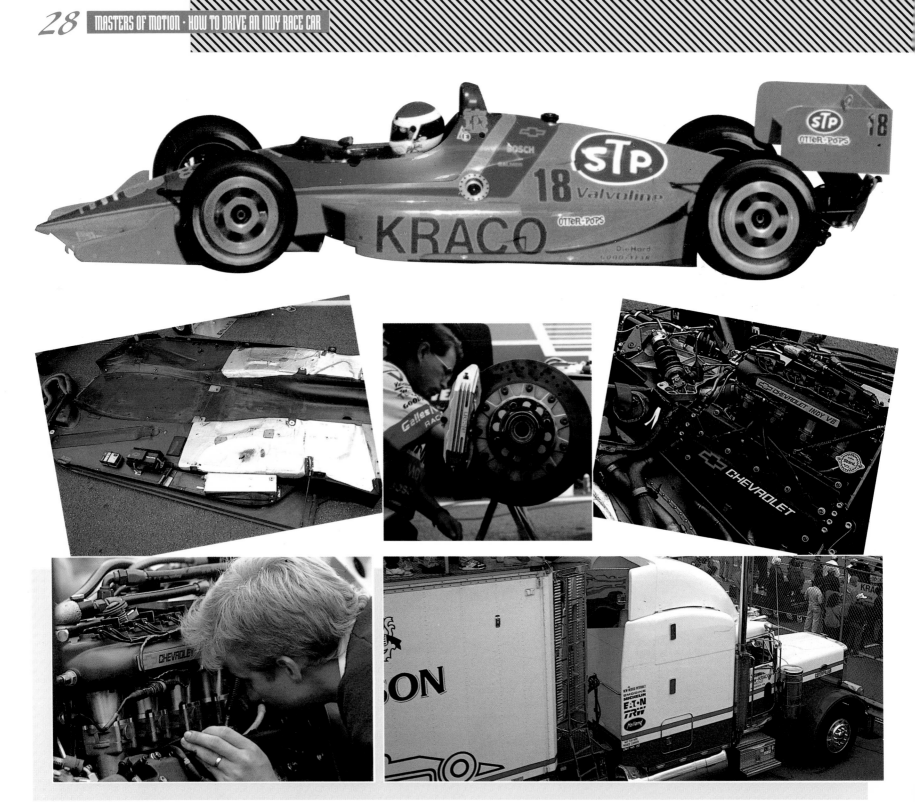

WHAT DOES IT COST TO RACE AN INDY CAR?

It costs money, and plenty of it. The average family can expect to spend about 61¢ per mile to buy, maintain, and operate a four-door sedan. Racing Indy cars competitively, however, costs team owners a little more. More on the order of $1,100 per mile, and even that figure keeps going up. If you plan to start your own team, here are some of the costs you can expect.

Chassis: The list price for a "rolling" chassis is $310,000. That includes body, suspension, and steering, but not the engine. It also fails to include the superspeedway kit, which is both a must and another $30,000. Most teams buy two or three cars, but for argument's sake, let's just say you'll try to make do with one.

Wheels: The rolling chassis comes with four wheels, but you'll need at least a dozen more sets. That's 48 wheels at $2,500 per wheel, or a budget line of $120,000.

Engines: You need six to ten engines per car, and each engine costs $100,000 to $125,000. If you do the math, it works out to about a million dollars just for engines. And they wear out every 500 miles or so, which means you'll have to add another $20,000 for each rebuilding job.

Tires: You need seven sets of tires for each of the seventeen IndyCar-sanctioned races—except for the two 500-mile races, when you'll need eleven sets. You also need tires for testing and for practicing between races. At $600-$750 per set, the cost adds up.

Spare Parts: Figure on $400,000 worth.

Transporter: Included in this long-distance hauler is room for two cars as well as a fully equipped machine shop. If you want a nice one, pencil in $500,000.

Team Costs: You also need engineers, mechanics, a team manager, transporter drivers—and, of course, someone to race your multimillion-dollar car for you. None of these people come cheap. There are salaries; travel, lodging, and food expenses; insurance payments; pension plans; and $500 more if you decide to spring for team T-shirts.

BACK TO THE TRACK

The starter motor turns the engine over, waking it up with a piston-pounding, jackhammer roar. As I pull out of pit row, I squeeze power and shift quickly from first through second and third. Pulling out onto the track, I'm already in fourth gear. All right. Now fifth, and the first turn. Nerve, nerve. Think fearless.

I wait, wait, wait—and then turn in hard and late. But it's too hard, and I can feel the car starting to oversteer. The rear tires want to pull out, and there's a squeal as they lose some grip.

Power! Power! Squeeze power!

I do, and the car rights itself as it comes hurtling out of the turn. Under this kind of speed, the steering wheel shakes, and so do I. Be tough. Here comes another turn. Get it right. Get the rhythm. Drift to the outside, trail the throttle. Wait, wait. Turn! Squeeze power. Clip the apex. Straighten. Drift to the wall.

Good one. Good one! But you're letting up as you come out of the turn. Watch your exit speed. Build on it. Go faster. Faster. Fast is everything.

My brain says go faster, but when I'm not looking, my body eases up. I step on the accelerator again.

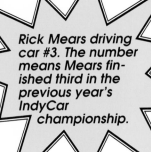

Rick Mears driving car #3. The number means Mears finished third in the previous year's IndyCar championship.

Riding this low to the ground in an open cockpit, the speed seems much, much faster than it does inside a passenger car. The track itself is a blur, and with no other cars around, it's hard to know how fast I should be going. With Al's constant urging, though, I pick up speed, and my lap times keep getting faster. Finally, Al calls me in.

Not bad. Did you notice your exit speeds improving? We were clocking you at one-fifty coming out of Turn Three. But I noticed that you never took the car into sixth gear.

"One-fifty seemed plenty fast."

Maybe now, but you've got to bear down. Trust the car. There are a dozen guys out here whose only job is to make sure that this machine performs for you.

"Don't you ever worry about crashing?"

The only time I think about it is afterward. One of my engineers once told me that when I'm running well, I drive the car so fast that the tires come very, very, very close to losing their grip in the turns. But that's the point of racing—to come very, very, very close to the edge and not cross over it. The ability to dance that fine line is the difference between a champion and an also-ran. You just won't be competitive in the race tomorrow at anything less than top speed, and on this track, we're talking one-eighty on the straightaways, fella.

"What do you mean, race?"

Whaddya mean whaddya mean? That's what we do here, pal. Get some rest. You've got a big day tomorrow.

RACE DAY

Race day. Time to make the final adjustments to the setup.

"Didn't we finish with the adjustments yesterday?"

We never *finish* with the adjustments. We'll probably even make some during the pit stops, but there's only so much you can do in nine seconds.

"I thought full pit stops took fifteen seconds."

To fill the fuel cell, yes. But it takes only six seconds to change the tires. So while the re-fuelers are finishing up, there are nine seconds to make setup adjustments.

"What's going on with the fuel cell?"

The mechanics are moving the fuel pickup to the right side of the cell.

"Why?"

Think for a minute. When you're going down a straightaway, where's the fuel?

"In the cell?"

Sure, but where in the cell? It's in the bottom, right?

"Right."

So where is it when you're turning left on an oval?

"I get it. When I'm turning left, the same centrifugal force that pulls me to the right also pulls the fuel over to the right side of the cell. That's really clever, putting the pickup there."

RACE WEEKEND

THURSDAY:
After the transporter arrives and is unloaded, the car is pushed over to the technical inspection tent, where officials take measurements to make sure its chassis meets IndyCar specifications for safety and competitiveness. The tub is the part of the car that actually has its serial number officially entered into the race.

FRIDAY:
During a morning practice session, drivers get their first opportunity to see how well their cars handle on the track. Team engineers use the Pi system to monitor each car's performance. Then they make adjustments and test the car again during a second practice session in the afternoon.

SATURDAY:
There's a final practice session in the early morning before qualifying begins that afternoon. The lap times posted by drivers during qualifying determine the starting grid for the race. The fastest qualifier wins the inside spot in the first row, called the pole position.

Every little bit helps. Even with all the electronics on board, the engineers still expect a 1/2 to 2 percent error in their fuel consumption calculations during a race. That can mean as much as a gallon of fuel, so the engineers have to dance just as fine a line as the driver. The really good ones can finish a race with less than a gallon left in the cell.

"Why not put in a few extra gallons, just to make sure?"

It takes about 0.4 second for a gallon of methanol to flow from the pit tank into the fuel cell. So figure it out. At racing speeds, an extra 0.4 second in the pit means falling another 100 feet behind.

"But if you cut it too close, you don't finish. You lose."

That's why we hire the best engineers and hope they know what they're doing. Fortunately, most of them do.

Racing Strategy

Ready for some racing strategy now? We'll begin with superspeedways, because they're simpler. At tracks like Indianapolis, you run the car flat out—no braking, no downshifting, nothing. Just full throttle the entire race. A Number Ten pedal, it's called, which means 100 percent floored.

"If you're going full out all the time, how do you pass someone? I mean, if you're already at a Number Ten pedal, you can't accelerate, can you?"

The most common way to pass on a superspeedway is called drafting. To draft a car means to drive so closely behind it that the two of you seem about to touch. When you're that close, you get to ride in the wake of the car in front of you, where there's less air resistance. As a result, you need only a Number Nine pedal to keep up.

Less air, though, also means less downforce and reduced cornering ability, because you lose some aerodynamic performance. So what you want to do is draft on the straightaways, and then just as you're entering a turn, pull down to the inside, pick up some clean air, go back to a Number Ten pedal, and slingshot

Pit fuel tank

past the car in front of you. On short ovals like this one, however, your main concern is traffic.

"*What do you mean, traffic? Are we racing at rush hour or something?*"

Yeah, only with no lanes and no stoplights. The traffic comes from cars that have been lapped, which you'll be if you don't start driving a little faster. On a circuit as short as this one, the leaders spend most of their time weaving in and out of traffic that may be one, two, or three laps behind them.

In addition to slowing you down, traffic also

poses some aerodynamic problems, because all those cars really mess up the airflow around the wings. We call any kind of turbulence dirty air, and believe me, there's plenty of dirty air in traffic. The sidepods have been designed to clean up some of it, but you'll always have down-force problems when you're stuck behind a pack of cars.

As far as this particular track is concerned, my advice is as follows: Go fast. Besides that, the inside of Turn Three seems a little bumpy, so I'd take a slightly higher than normal line through it. You might also want to touch the brakes a bit going in, but on the other turns, just trail throttle and the tires will scrub off the excess speed by themselves.

"*When do I pit?*"

According to IndyCar rules, you have to average at least 1.8 miles per gallon. Because this is a 200-mile race, everybody gets 200 divided by 1.8, or about 111 gallons of methanol. The fuel cell capacity is 40 gallons, so you'll have to pit twice. We'll tell you when. Understand?

"A *no-brainer*."

Ready to rock 'n' roll?

"*Yeah, I think so. Yeah! Let's do it! Just show me that Number Ten pedal!*"

All right! Good attitude. Climb on in. Seat belts tight? O.K. Start him up, boys!

RACE DAY

At 7:00 a.m., the track gates open, and by 7:30 a.m., crews have begun to fill the fuel tanks in the pits. At 10:00 a.m., IndyCar officials meet with the chief mechanics. An hour later, there's a drivers meeting. At 12:15 p.m., the cars are rolled out into the starting grid. And at 12:30 p.m., the drivers are introduced.

Drivers grid up for the start of an Indy 500. The race is run annually on Memorial Day weekend, but the pre-race qualifying takes up the entire month of May. Thirty-three cars qualify; often less than half finish.

THE INDY 500

THE INDY 500

Two hundred laps around a 2.5-mile oval. The math is simple, and so is the race. You run flat out for nearly three hours, from the green flag to the checkered, slowing down only for pit stops. The turns are so wide that you ignore them. It's Number Ten pedal all the way. To win this race, you should be pushing 235 miles an hour down the straightaways. Speed. That's what the Indianapolis 500 is all about. It couldn't be simpler.

The men who built the Indianapolis Motor Speedway in 1909 thought they were constructing a new testing facility for the country's surging automobile industry. But they also decided to take advantage of the growing interest in motor sports by staging a few races. The first surface they laid at the track—a mixture of crushed rock and tar—was designed to handle speeds of up to 75 miles per hour. But even in 1909, the best cars could run faster than that, so there were a number of accidents. A few months later, the owners decided to resurface the IMS with 3.2 million bricks at the then-hefty cost of $200,000.

Eighteen months later, on May 30, 1911, Ray Harroun won the first Indianapolis 500. It took him just under seven hours to win the race, riding at an average speed of 74.59 miles per hour. In 1925, Peter DePaolo became the first driver to average better than 100 miles per hour when he won the race in 4:56. And of course, the speeds have kept increasing. Today, it takes lap speeds over 220 miles per hour to win the pole position at Indy.

The Race

Once again I find myself strapped into this land rocket, a small nosecone sitting on top of a big engine with wheels. With twenty-two cars in the starting grid, the noise is louder than a jet engine. But the earplugs are working well, and I can hear Al over the radio fine.

The pace car is moving out. Follow it.

The cars in front of me follow the pace car, and I follow them. But suddenly everybody stops driving in a straight line.

"Al, buddy, what's going on? Why are the other drivers weaving their cars all over the track?"

They're scrubbing their tires, and you should be scrubbing yours, too. Weaving back and forth like that helps warm the tires up to their running temperature.

So I start weaving back and forth, scrubbing my tires. After a couple of laps, traffic lights on the side of the track turn from yellow to green, which means that the green flag is coming. The race is about to start, so it's gut-check time. I haven't taken the car into sixth gear yet, and I'm not sure that any sane person would. But as we pull out of Turn Three, I know it's too late to worry about that now. The pace car's approaching the starting line, and here . . . comes . . . the . . . green . . . flag. NOW!

COLD TIRES

WARM TIRES

TIRES AT RUNNING TEMPERATURE

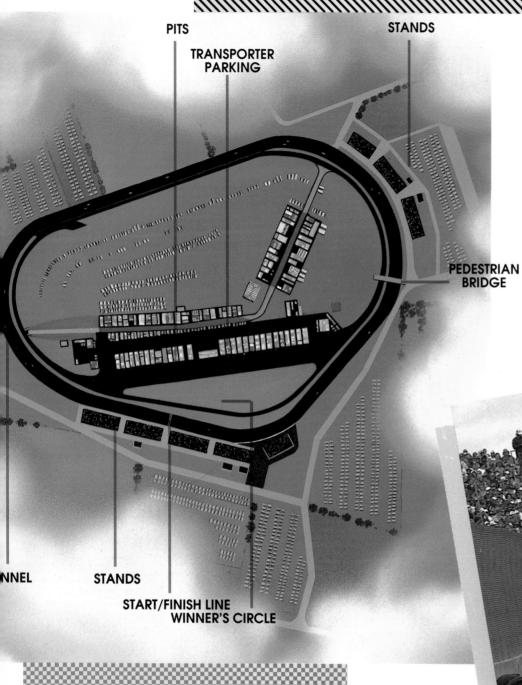

PITS

TRANSPORTER
PARKING

STANDS

PEDESTRIAN
BRIDGE

NNEL

STANDS

START/FINISH LINE
WINNER'S CIRCLE

THE TRACK

Full Throttle

I floor the accelerator and feel the g-forces immediately push me back into the carbon-fiber seat. Whatever the crew did to the setup this morning is really making the car move. But even at this speed, cars are already passing me by. One, two, three, and I haven't even turned yet.

Shift! Shift! Go faster!

Without realizing it, I had picked my foot up off the throttle. I was at a Number Three pedal when I should have been running a Number Eight or Nine at least At Al's urging, I plant my right foot and take Turn One. The tires squeal at the turn-in point. But the grip holds and I add power, avoiding the oversteer. Popping out of the turn, I hold my exit speed, and suddenly the cars aren't pulling away from me quite as fast.

Then it happens. A car well in front of me drops wheels inside of Turn Two and skids up the track toward the outside wall. Two trailing cars can't help but plow into him, and a third is taken out by a flying sidepod. I brake hard and swing down to the inside, avoiding the wreckage.

Within seconds, the IndyCar Safety Team is on the scene—two trucks overflowing with fire-fighting and medical equipment. Everyone's O.K., but the impact has totaled the cars, taking four drivers out of the race. The yellow flag comes out. If it's any consolation to them, those four drivers have just catapulted me from

twenty-second into eighteenth place. I toggle the radio mike.

"Hey, Al, what happened up there?"

Pretty simple, really. A driver just hadn't scrubbed his tires well enough. When he tried to take that turn at top speed, his grip failed to hold. That's why you've got to be careful at the start of a race. You don't want to open up too quickly, because the car needs time to adjust to the track and settle in, especially the tires.

"You mean it's good to go slow?"

Don't start getting any ideas. You just think about going fast. I'll tell you when to slow down.

Under the yellow flag, the race tightens up. I may be in last place, but at least I haven't been lapped yet. In about ten minutes, the track is cleared, the green flag comes out, and we're back to racing. I try to hang tough and stick to the tail of the car in front of me. But with each turn, I fall farther behind. Soon enough, I get lapped. And then a little later, I get lapped again.

What are you doing out there? This is a race, not a Sunday drive in the country. Be aggressive! Ride the edge. Fearless. Think fearless!

Faster! Faster!

With each prod from Al, I squeeze the power a little more, but it's hard to hold onto the speed. Trying to forget how fast I'm going, I glue my eyes to the pack in front of me and try not to look at the walls flying past. Trail throttle, turn, squeeze power, track out. Touch the brakes. Cut to the apex. Power. Slingshot out. At first, I let up a little coming out of the turns and lose ground on the straightaways. But then I start tucking the turns a little tighter, waiting better at the turn-in point, and my exit speeds pick up. Slowly, I start to gain on the pack. I'm not about to set any records, but I'm not getting lapped as quickly, either.

And I am getting awfully close to that black car in front of me. I go from a Number Eight pedal to a Number Nine.

You've got him, kid. Watch your line through Turn Two. Keep the power on. Now take a lower line through Turn Three and really punch that exit speed.

I run within what seems like millimeters of the outside wall, wait until the last possible second, then steer hard down into Turn Three, dropping under the line the black car is taking.

Now power! Squeeze power! Go to the Number Ten!

Bearing down on the clipping point, I pull into some clean air and really feel the extra downforce stick the car to the track. This is it. I go to a Number Ten pedal and keep it there. My neck strains against the helmet strap, but then I pass the apex and face the next crisis. The car starts skidding instead of drifting to the track-out point. But somehow I keep control and end up sweeping past the outside wall with my foot still riding a Number Ten pedal.

"Al! Al! Where's the black car?"

In your wake, man. You just put him in your rearview mirror. You passed him!

"Wa-HOO!"

You're starting to run a little low on fuel, though, so come on in.

"Now? But I'm cooking *now*."

So you pass one car and all of a sudden you're a hero? Get real. Tell me, how's the car handling?

"*Great. Maybe a slight bit of oversteer.*"

Message received and understood. All right, bring it in.

Pit Stop

I pull into the pit and brake tight on the T-marks. Even before I'm completely still, the six-man pit crew jumps over the fire wall and attacks the car. The compressor coupling pops on, and a second later the air jack's got me half a foot off the ground. The impact wrenches chatter violently as four tires spin off and another four spin on.

We're reducing the rear tire pressure to give you a little more grip and help out with the oversteer. We're also adjusting the front wing. Now listen. When the air jack cuts out, you'll bounce. So don't worry. But don't wait either. Here's the bounce.

Go!

A crew member works the air jack

COMPUTERS IN RACING

The engineer's best friend in Indy car racing is the onboard computer in the Pi Box. It records everything that happens to the car and then downloads that data to a laptop computer so it can be analyzed.

For example, the Pi Box reads engine rpm every 1/100 of a second. Therefore, in one second, the Pi Box takes 100 data readings. The oil temperature, however, is monitored only every 1/10 of a second, because it doesn't move up or down as quickly.

Racing teams keep records of Pi Box data from years back to help them prepare for races at tracks they've run on before. Studying the top speeds reached at a track in the past, for example, can help engineers determine the best gearing configuration for an upcoming race.

Racing Again

The new tires scream as I peel out. Al's team has come through again. Right away, I feel the difference in handling and stick. With these fresh tires, I ease off a bit going into the turns, but as fast as I'm running on the straightaways, the tires warm up quickly.

Faster, faster. Fast is *everything*. Push it to the edge!

At the speed I'm making now, I start to move up. Coming down the straightaway between Turns Two and Three, I pull up behind the black car again and draft him. I'm so close that I can almost reach out and touch his rear wing. Trailing to a Number Eight pedal, I wait, wait, wait, then snap off hard to the inside of Turn Three. Too hard. I pull down past the black car, but the rear wheels are slipping. I punch the power. But it's not enough. I can't hold the line. I try to recover by turning into the spin. But then I hit a bump, and that spike load sends me out of control.

Lock it in! Lock it in! If you spin, lock it in!

I jump on the brakes and the clutch and hold on. I feel the car twisting, and the next thing I know I'm on the infield grass, having gone from one-sixty to zero in what seems like two seconds flat. Except for a couple of sore spots where the seat belts grabbed me, I'm fine. I wish I could remember how to breathe, though.

It's Over!

Well, that was a six o'clock news highlight for sure. Glad to see you came out of it O.K. Welcome to the club.

"What club is that? I didn't even finish half the race."

Yeah, but you did something a lot more important. You pushed the car to the limit of its performance—past that limit, really—and rode the bubble, even if it was for only a second or two. That's what matters.

So you fell off. It happens. But at least you've been there. You've had the nerve to find out what it's like. You went fast. And fast is everything.

GLOSSARIZED INDEX

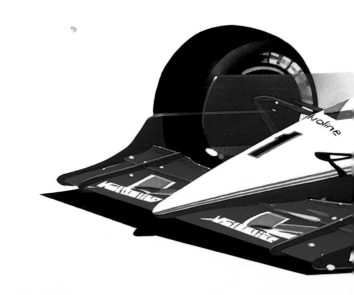

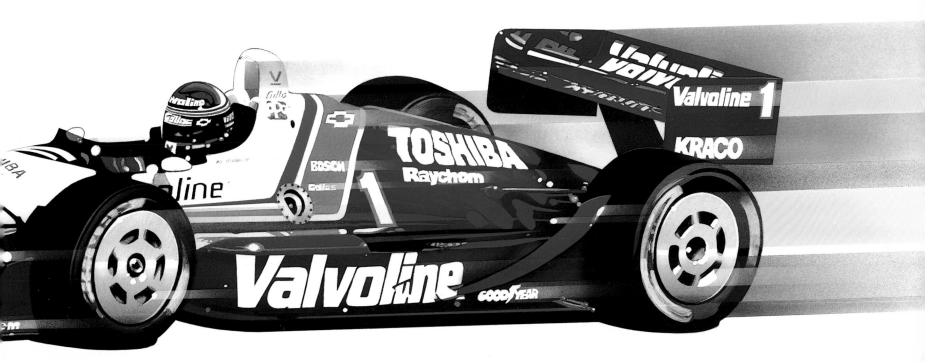

X-ray Vision Series

Each title in the series is 8½" × 11", 48 pages, with four-color photographs and illustrations.

Looking Inside the Brain
Ron Schultz
$9.95 paper

Looking Inside Cartoon Animation
Ron Schultz
$9.95 paper

Looking Inside Sports Aerodynamics
Ron Schultz
$9.95 paper

The Quill Hedgehog Adventures Series

Green fiction for young readers. Each title in the series is written by John Waddington-Feather and illustrated by Doreen Edmond.

Quill's Adventures in the Great Beyond
Book One
5½" × 8½", 96 pages, $5.95 paper

Quill's Adventures in Wasteland
Book Two
5½" × 8½", 132 pages, $5.95 paper

Quill's Adventures in Grozzieland
Book Three
5½" × 8½", 132 pages, $5.95 paper

Masters of Motion Series

Each title in the series is 10¼" × 9", 48 pages, with four-color photographs and illustrations.

How to Drive an Indy Race Car
David Rubel
$9.95 paper

How to Fly a 747
Tim Paulson
$9.95 paper

How to Fly the Space Shuttle
Russell Shorto
$9.95 paper   (avail. 11/92)

The Extremely Weird Series

All of the titles in the Extremely Weird Series are written by Sarah Lovett, are 8½" × 11", 48 pages, and $9.95 paperbacks.

Extremely Weird Bats

Extremely Weird Birds

Extremely Weird Endangered Species

Extremely Weird Fishes

Extremely Weird Frogs

Extremely Weird Insects

Extremely Weird Primates

Extremely Weird Reptiles

Extremely Weird Sea Creatures

Extremely Weird Spiders

Other Titles of Interest

Kids Explore America's Hispanic Heritage
Westridge Young Writers Workshop
7" × 9", 112 pages, illustrations
$7.95 paper

Rads, Ergs, and Cheeseburgers
The Kids' Guide to Energy and the Environment
Bill Yanda
Illustrated by Michael Taylor
7" × 9", 108 pages, two-color illustrations
$12.95 paper

The Kids' Environment Book
What's Awry and Why
Anne Pedersen
Illustrated by Sally Blakemore
7" × 9", 192 pages, two-color illustrations
$13.95 paper
For Ages 10 and Up

The Indian Way
Learning to Communicate with Mother Earth
Gary McLain
Paintings by Gary McLain
Illustrations by Michael Taylor
7" × 9", 114 pages, two-color illustrations
$9.95 paper

The Kidding Around Travel Series

All of the titles listed below are 64 pages and $9.95 except for *Kidding Around the National Parks of the Southwest* and *Kidding Around Spain*, which are 108 pages and $12.95.

Kidding Around Atlanta

Kidding Around Boston

Kidding Around Chicago

Kidding Around the Hawaiian Islands

Kidding Around London

Kidding Around Los Angeles

Kidding Around the National Parks of the Southwest

Kidding Around New York City

Kidding Around Paris

Kidding Around Philadelphia

Kidding Around San Diego

Kidding Around San Francisco

Kidding Around Santa Fe

Kidding Around Seattle

Kidding Around Spain

Kidding Around Washington, D.C.

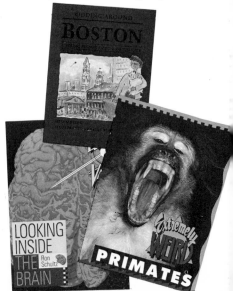

ORDERING INFORMATION Your books will be sent to you via UPS (for U.S. destinations). UPS will not deliver to a P.O. Box; please give us a street address. Include $3.75 for the first item ordered and $.50 for each additional item to cover shipping and handling costs. For airmail within the U.S., enclose $4.00. All foreign orders will be shipped surface rate; please enclose $3.00 for the first item and $1.00 for each additional item. Please inquire about foreign airmail rates.

METHOD OF PAYMENT Your order may be paid by check, money order, or credit card. We cannot be responsible for cash sent through the mail. All payments must be made in U.S. dollars drawn on a U.S. bank. Canadian postal money orders in U.S. dollars are acceptable. For VISA, MasterCard, or American Express orders, include your card number, expiration date, and your signature, or call (800) 888-7504. Books ordered on American Express cards can be shipped only to the billing address of the cardholder. Sorry, no C.O.D.'s. Residents of sunny New Mexico, add 5.875% tax to the total.

Address all orders and inquiries to: **John Muir Publications**, P.O. Box 613, Santa Fe, NM 87504, (505) 982-4078, (800) 888-7504.